Contents

Italian Sausage Soup

SAUSAGE MEATBALLS

   1 pound bulk mild Italian sausage, casings removed

   ½ cup plain dry bread crumbs

   ¼ cup grated Parmesan cheese, plus additional for garnish

   ¼ cup milk

   1 egg

   ½ teaspoon dried basil

   ½ teaspoon black pepper

   ¼ teaspoon garlic salt

SOUP

   4 cups hot chicken broth

   1 tablespoon tomato paste

   2 cloves garlic, minced

   ¼ teaspoon red pepper flakes

   ½ cup uncooked mini pasta shells*

   1 bag (10 ounces) baby spinach

Or use other tiny pasta, such as ditalini (mini tubes) or farfallini (mini bowties).

1. Combine sausage, bread crumbs, ¼ cup cheese, milk, egg, basil, black pepper and garlic salt in medium bowl. Shape into marble-size meatballs.

2. Combine broth, tomato paste, garlic and red pepper flakes in **CROCK-POT®** slow cooker. Add meatballs. Cover; cook on **LOW 5 to 6 hours.**

3. Add pasta 30 minutes before serving. When pasta is tender, stir in spinach. Sprinkle with additional Parmesan cheese.

Makes 8 servings

New Mexican Green Chile Pork Stew

1½ **pounds boneless pork shoulder, cut into 1-inch cubes**
2 **medium baking potatoes or sweet potatoes, peeled and cut into large chunks**
1 **cup chopped onion**
1 **can (4 ounces) diced green chiles**
1 **cup frozen corn**
2 **teaspoons sugar**
2 **teaspoons cumin or chili powder**
1 **teaspoon dried oregano**
1 **jar (16 ounces) salsa verde (green salsa)**
   Hot cooked rice
¼ **cup chopped fresh cilantro**

1. Place pork, potatoes, onion, chiles and corn into **CROCK-POT**® slow cooker. Stir sugar, cumin and oregano into salsa and pour over pork and vegetables. Stir gently to mix.

2. Cover; cook on **LOW 6 to 8 hours** or on **HIGH 4 to 5 hours** or until pork is tender. Serve stew over hot rice and garnish with cilantro.

makes 6 servings

Tip: Root vegetables such as potatoes can sometimes take longer to cook in a **CROCK-POT**® slow cooker than meat. Place evenly cut vegetables on the bottom or along the sides of the **CROCK-POT**® slow cooker when possible.

Curried Sweet Potato and Carrot Soup

2 medium to large sweet potatoes, peeled and cut into ¾-inch dice (about 5 cups)

2 cups baby carrots

1 small onion, chopped

¾ teaspoon curry powder

½ teaspoon salt

½ teaspoon black pepper

½ teaspoon ground cinnamon

¼ teaspoon ground ginger

4 cups chicken broth

1 tablespoon maple syrup

¾ cup half-and-half

Candied ginger (optional)

1. Place sweet potatoes, carrots, onion, curry powder, salt, pepper, cinnamon and ginger in **CROCK-POT®** slow cooker. Add broth. Stir well to combine. Cover; cook on **LOW 7 to 8 hours.**

2. Process soup, 1 cup at a time, in blender or food processor until smooth. Return soup to **CROCK-POT®** slow cooker. (Alternatively, use immersion blender to purée soup.) Add maple syrup and half-and-half. Add salt and pepper, if desired. Cover; cook on **HIGH 15 minutes** to reheat. Serve in bowls and garnish with candied ginger.

makes 8 servings

Tip: If desired, add a teaspoon of chicken soup base along with the broth for richer flavor.

Sweet and Sour Brisket Stew

  1 jar (12 ounces) chili sauce

  ¼ cup beef broth

1½ to 2 tablespoons packed dark brown sugar

1½ tablespoons fresh lemon juice

  1 tablespoon Dijon mustard

  ¼ teaspoon paprika

  ½ teaspoon salt

  ¼ teaspoon black pepper

  1 well-trimmed beef brisket, cut into 1-inch pieces*

  2 large carrots, cut into ½-inch slices

  1 small onion, chopped

  1 garlic clove, minced

  1 tablespoon all-purpose flour (optional)

Beef brisket has a heavy layer of fat, which some supermarkets trim off. If the meat is trimmed, buy 2½ pounds; if not, purchase 4 pounds, then trim and discard excess fat.

1. Combine chili sauce, broth, 1½ tablespoons brown sugar, lemon juice, mustard, paprika, salt and pepper in **CROCK-POT®** slow cooker. (Add remaining sugar, if desired, after tasting.)

2. Add beef, carrots, onion and garlic; stir well to coat. Cover; cook on **LOW 8 hours.**

3. If thicker gravy is desired, combine 1 tablespoon flour and 3 tablespoons cooking liquid in small bowl. Add to **CROCK-POT®** slow cooker. Cover; cook on **HIGH 10 minutes** or until thickened.

makes 6 to 8 servings

Celery-Leek Bisque

3 bunches leeks (about 3 pounds), trimmed and well rinsed

2 medium stalks celery, sliced

1 medium carrot, sliced

3 cloves garlic, minced

2 cans (about 14 ounces each) chicken broth

1 package (8 ounces) cream cheese with garlic and herbs

2 cups half-and-half, plus more for garnish

Salt and black pepper

Fresh basil leaves (optional)

1. Combine leeks, celery, carrot, garlic and broth in **CROCK-POT**® slow cooker. Cover; cook on **LOW 8 hours** or on **HIGH 4 hours.**

2. Process mixture in blender, 1 cup at a time, until smooth, returning batches to **CROCK-POT**® slow cooker as they are processed. Add cream cheese to last batch in blender; purée until smooth. Stir cream cheese mixture and 2 cups half-and-half into soup. Season with salt and pepper. Serve immediately or cool to room temperature and refrigerate in airtight container (flavors intensify overnight). Reheat before serving. Garnish with additional half-and-half and basil leaves.

Makes 4 to 6 servings

Tip: It is very important to rinse leeks thoroughly before using. The gritty sand in which leeks are grown can become trapped between the layers of leaves and can be difficult to see. Cut trimmed leeks in half lengthwise and submerge in several inches of cool water several times to rinse off any trapped sand.

Asian Beef Stew

 2 onions, cut into ¼-inch slices

1½ pounds round steak, sliced thinly across the grain

 2 stalks celery, sliced

 2 carrots, peeled and sliced or 1 cup peeled baby carrots

 1 cup sliced mushrooms

 1 cup orange juice

 1 cup beef broth

 ⅓ cup hoisin sauce

 2 tablespoons cornstarch

 1 to 2 teaspoons Chinese five-spice powder or curry powder

 1 cup frozen peas

    Hot cooked rice

    Chopped fresh cilantro (optional)

1. Place onions, beef, celery, carrots and mushrooms in **CROCK-POT**® slow cooker.

2. Combine orange juice, broth, hoisin sauce, cornstarch and five-spice powder in small bowl. Pour into **CROCK-POT**® slow cooker. Cover; cook on **HIGH 5 hours** or until beef is tender.

3. Stir in peas. Cook 20 minutes or until peas are tender. Serve with rice. Garnish with cilantro.

makes 6 servings

Chicken Tortilla Soup

4 boneless, skinless chicken thighs

2 cans (15 ounces each) diced tomatoes

½ to 1 cup chicken broth, divided

1 can (4 ounces) chopped mild green chiles, drained

1 yellow onion, diced

2 cloves garlic, minced

1 teaspoon ground cumin

Salt and black pepper, to taste

4 corn tortillas, sliced into ¼-inch strips

2 tablespoons chopped fresh cilantro

½ cup (2 ounces) shredded Monterey Jack cheese

1 avocado, peeled, diced and tossed with lime juice to prevent browning

Lime wedges

1. Place chicken in **CROCK-POT®** slow cooker. Combine tomatoes, ½ cup broth, chiles, onion, garlic and cumin in small bowl. Pour mixture over chicken. Cover; cook on **HIGH 3 hours** or until chicken is tender.

2. Remove chicken from **CROCK-POT®** slow cooker. Shred with two forks. Return to cooking liquid. Adjust seasonings, adding more broth if necessary.

3. Just before serving, add tortillas and cilantro to **CROCK-POT®** slow cooker. Stir to blend. Serve in soup bowls, topping each serving with cheese, avocado and a squeeze of lime juice.

makes 4 to 6 servings

Chipotle Chicken Stew

1 pound boneless, skinless chicken thighs, cut into cubes
1 can (about 15 ounces) navy beans, rinsed and drained
1 can (about 15 ounces) black beans, rinsed and drained
1 can (about 14 ounces) crushed tomatoes, undrained
1½ cups chicken broth
½ cup orange juice
1 medium onion, diced
1 chipotle pepper in adobo sauce, minced
1 teaspoon salt
1 teaspoon ground cumin
1 bay leaf
Cilantro sprigs (optional)

1. Combine chicken, beans, tomatoes, broth, orange juice, onion, chipotle pepper, salt, cumin and bay leaf in **CROCK-POT®** slow cooker.

2. Cover; cook on **LOW 7 to 8 hours** or on **HIGH 3½ to 4 hours.** Remove bay leaf before serving. Garnish with cilantro sprigs, if desired.

makes 6 servings

Easy Beef Stew

1½ to 2 pounds beef stew meat, cut into 1-inch cubes
4 medium potatoes, cut into 1-inch cubes
4 carrots, cut into 1½-inch pieces or 4 cups baby carrots
1 medium onion, cut into 8 wedges
2 cans (8 ounces each) tomato sauce
1 teaspoon salt
½ teaspoon black pepper
Chopped parsley (optional)

Combine all ingredients in 4½-quart in **CROCK-POT®** slow cooker. Cover; cook on **LOW 8 to 10 hours** or until vegetables are tender. Garnish as desired.

makes 6 to 8 servings

CHIPOTLE CHICKEN STEW

French Lentil Rice Soup

6 cups chicken or vegetable broth

1 cup lentils, rinsed and sorted

2 medium carrots, finely diced

1 small onion, finely chopped

2 stalks celery, finely diced

3 tablespoons uncooked rice

2 tablespoons minced garlic

1 teaspoon herbes de Provence or dried thyme

½ teaspoon salt

⅛ teaspoon white or black pepper

¼ cup whipping cream or sour cream (optional)

¼ cup chopped fresh parsley (optional)

1. Stir broth, lentils, carrots, onion, celery, rice, garlic, herbes de Provence, salt and pepper in **CROCK-POT®** slow cooker. Cover; cook on **LOW 8 hours** or on **HIGH 4 to 5 hours.**

2. Remove 1½ cups soup; process in blender or food processor until almost smooth.* Stir puréed soup back into **CROCK-POT®** slow cooker.

3. Divide soup evenly among four serving bowls. Garnish each serving with 1 tablespoon cream and 1 tablespoon chopped parsley.

Makes 4 servings

Use caution when processing hot liquids in blender. Vent lid of blender and cover with clean kitchen towel as directed by manufacturer.

Sweet Potato Stew

- 1 cup chopped onion
- 1 cup chopped celery
- 1 cup grated sweet potato
- 1 cup vegetable broth or water
- 2 slices bacon, crisp-cooked and crumbled
- 1 cup half-and-half
  Black pepper
- ¼ cup minced fresh parsley

1. Place onion, celery, sweet potato, broth and bacon in **CROCK-POT®** slow cooker. Cover; cook on **LOW 6 hours.**

2. Turn **CROCK-POT®** slow cooker to **HIGH.** Add enough half-and-half to **CROCK-POT®** slow cooker to reach desired consistency. Cook, uncovered, on **HIGH 30 minutes** or until heated through.

3. Season to taste with pepper. Stir in parsley.

Makes 4 servings

Creamy Crab Bisque

- 4 cups whipping cream
- 3 cups fresh crabmeat, flaked and picked over
- 3 tablespoons unsalted butter
- 2 teaspoons grated lemon peel
- 1 teaspoon lemon juice
- ½ teaspoon ground nutmeg
- ¼ teaspoon ground allspice
- 3 tablespoons dry red wine
- ½ cup prepared mandlen (soup nuts), ground into crumbs*

Mandlen are small nugget-like crackers made from matzo meal, available in the supermarket ethnic foods aisle.

1. Combine cream, crab, butter, lemon peel, lemon juice, nutmeg and allspice in 4½- to 6-quart **CROCK-POT®** slow cooker. Stir well to combine. Cover; cook on **LOW 1 to 2 hours.**

2. Stir in wine. Add mandlen crumbs to thicken soup and stir again. Continue cooking on **LOW 10 minutes.**

makes 6 to 8 servings

SWEET POTATO STEW

Cannellini Minestrone

- 4 cups chicken broth
- 1 can (about 14 ounces) diced tomatoes, undrained
- 1 can (12 ounces) tomato-vegetable juice
- 2 cups escarole, cut into ribbons
- 1 cup chopped green onions
- 1 cup chopped carrots
- 1 cup chopped celery
- 1 cup chopped potatoes
- ¼ cup dried cannellini beans, sorted and rinsed
- 2 tablespoons chopped fresh chives
- 1 tablespoon chopped fresh flat-leaf parsley
- ¼ teaspoon salt
- ¼ teaspoon black pepper
- 2 ounces uncooked ditalini pasta

1. Place all ingredients except pasta in **CROCK-POT®** slow cooker. Stir well to combine. Cover; cook on **LOW 6 to 8 hours** or on **HIGH 4 to 6 hours.**

2. Add ditalini and stir again. Cover; cook on **LOW 20 minutes.**

makes 6 servings

Hearty Lentil and Root Vegetable Stew

   2 cans (about 14 ounces each) chicken broth
1½ cups turnips, cut into 1-inch cubes
   1 cup dried red lentils, rinsed and sorted
   2 medium carrots, cut into 1-inch pieces
   1 medium onion, cut into ½-inch wedges
   1 medium red bell pepper, cut into 1-inch pieces
  ½ teaspoon dried oregano
  ⅛ teaspoon red pepper flakes
   1 tablespoon olive oil
  ½ teaspoon salt
   4 slices bacon, crisp-cooked and crumbled
  ½ cup finely chopped green onions

1. Combine broth, turnips, lentils, carrots, onion, bell pepper, oregano and red pepper flakes in **CROCK-POT**® slow cooker. Stir to mix well. Cover; cook on **LOW 6 hours** or on **HIGH 3 hours** or until lentils are tender.

2. Stir in olive oil and salt. Sprinkle each serving with bacon and green onions.

makes 8 servings

Slow Cooker Cheese Soup

2 cans (10¾ ounces each) condensed cream of celery soup, undiluted
4 cups (16 ounces) shredded Cheddar cheese
1 teaspoon paprika, plus additional for garnish
1 teaspoon Worcestershire sauce
1¼ cups half-and-half
    Salt and black pepper
    Snipped chives

1. Combine soup, cheese, 1 teaspoon paprika and Worcestershire sauce in **CROCK-POT®** slow cooker. Cover; cook on **LOW 2 to 3 hours.**

2. Add half-and-half; stir until blended. Cover; cook on **LOW 20 minutes.** Season to taste with salt and pepper. Sprinkle with additional paprika and chives.

Makes 4 servings

Old-Fashioned Split Pea Soup

4 quarts chicken broth
2 pounds dried split peas
1 cup chopped ham
½ cup chopped onion
½ cup chopped celery
2 teaspoons salt
2 teaspoons black pepper

1. Place all ingredients in **CROCK-POT®** slow cooker; stir well to combine. Cover; cook on **LOW 8 to 10 hours** or on **HIGH 4 to 6 hours** or until peas are soft.

2. Mix with immersion blender on low speed until smooth.

makes 8 servings

SLOW COOKER CHEESE SOUP

Mushroom-Beef Stew

1 **pound beef stew meat**

1 **can (10¾ ounces) condensed cream of mushroom soup, undiluted**

2 **cans (4 ounces each) sliced mushrooms, drained**

1 **package (1 ounce) dry onion soup mix**

Hot cooked noodles

Combine all ingredients except noodles in 4½-quart **CROCK-POT®** slow cooker. Cover; cook on **LOW 8 to 10 hours.** Serve over noodles.

makes 4 servings